T0052707

THE HUMAN BODY

Fighting Disease

KATE BOEHM JEROME

PICTURE CREDITS
Cover: Linda S. Nye/Phototake. Pages 1, 15 (top), 16 (top), 17, 23, 25 (top) PhotoDisc®, pages 2–3 © Chris Collins/Corbis Stock Market; page 4 SPL/Photo Researchers, Inc.; page 5 © B. Toby/Stock Connection/PictureQuest; page 6 (top) Roy Botterell/gettyimages; page 6 (low left) © BSIP/Laurent/Science Source/Photo Researchers, Inc.; page 6 (low right) Laura Lane/gettyimages; page 7 © CNRI/Phototake; page 8 (top) Bonnie Cosgrove/SPL/Photo Researchers, Inc.; page 8 (low) Dr. Tony Brain/SPL/Photo Reseachers, Inc.; page 9 (top) © Oliver Meckes/Photo Researchers, Inc.; page 9 (mid) © Biophoto Assoc./Photo Reseachers, Inc.; page 9 (low) Manfred Kage/Peter Arnold, Inc.; page 10 (top) David Duprey/AP; page 10 (low) Pictor International/PictureQuest; page 11 (top) Mary Kate Denny/PhotoEdit/PictureQuest page 11 (low) David Young-Wolff/PhotoEdit/PictureQuest; pages 12, 27 (low left) KT Design; pages 13 (left), 20–21 art by Precision Graphics; page 13 (top right) Stephen Welstead/LWA/Corbis Stock Market; page 13 (low) EyeWire/gettyimages; page 14 Matthew Naythons; page 15 (low) H. Schwarzbach/Peter Arnold, Inc.; page 16 (low left) © James Webb/Phototake; page 16 (low right) Saturn Stills/SPL/Photo Researchers, Inc.; page 18 (top) George Bernard/SPL/Photo Researchers, Inc.; page 18 (low) Bettmann/CORBIS; page 19 St. Mary's Hospital Medical School/SPL/Photo Researchers, Inc.; page 20 (mid) © David Samuel Robbins/CORBIS; page 22 (left) ER Productions/CORBIS; page 22 (top right) Phototake; page 22 (low right) photo by Brad Bower, courtesy of Jewish Hospital, Louisville, Kentucky; page 24 © Impact Visuals/ Phototake; page 25 (low) Jon Feingersh/CORBIS; page 27 (top right) Wil & Deni McIntyre/Photo Researchers, Inc.; pages 28–29 Lloyd Wolf.

Back cover: (top to bottom) © Corbis Royalty Free Images, PhotoDisc®, © Digital Vision Ltd., PhotoDisc®, PhotoDisc®.

Neither the publisher nor the author shall be liable for any damage that may be caused or sustained or result from conducting any of the activities in this book without specifically following instructions, undertaking the activities without proper supervision, or failing to comply with the cautions contained in the book.

Cover photo: A model of the adenovirus, which causes respiratory infections in humans

Produced through the worldwide resources of the National Geographic Society, John M. Fahey, Jr., President and Chief Executive Officer; Gilbert M. Grosvenor, Chairman of the Board; Nina D. Hoffman, Executive Vice President and President, Books and School Publishing.

PREPARED BY NATIONAL GEOGRAPHIC SCHOOL PUBLISHING
Ericka Markman, Senior Vice President; Steve Mico, Editorial Director; Barbara Seeber, Editorial Manager; Lynda McMurray, Amy Sarver, Anita Schwartz, Project Editors; Roger B. Hirschland, Consulting Editor; Jim Hiscott, Design Manager; Karen Thompson, Art Director; Kristin Hanneman, Illustrations Manager; Diana Bourdrez, Tom DiGiovanni, Ruth Goldberg, Photo Editors; Christine Higgins, Photo Coordinator; Matt Wascavage, Manager of Publishing Services; Sean Philpotts, Production Coordinator.

Production: Clifton M. Brown III, Manufacturing and Quality Control.

CONSULTANT/REVIEWER
Rebecca L. Johnson, Biologist, Sioux Falls, South Dakota

PROGRAM DEVELOPMENT
Kate Boehm Jerome

BOOK DESIGN
Herman Adler Design

Copyright © 2003 National Geographic Society. All Rights Reserved. Reproduction in whole or in part of the contents without written permission from the publisher is prohibited.

National Geographic Society, National Geographic School Publishing, National Geographic Reading Expeditions, and the Yellow Border are trademarks of the National Geographic Society.

Published by the National Geographic Society
1145 17th Street, N.W.
Washington, D.C. 20036-4688

ISBN13: 978-0-7922-8865-7
ISBN10: 0-7922-8865-3

Printed in the U.S.A.

20 19 18
5 4 3 2

will be yours.

Contents

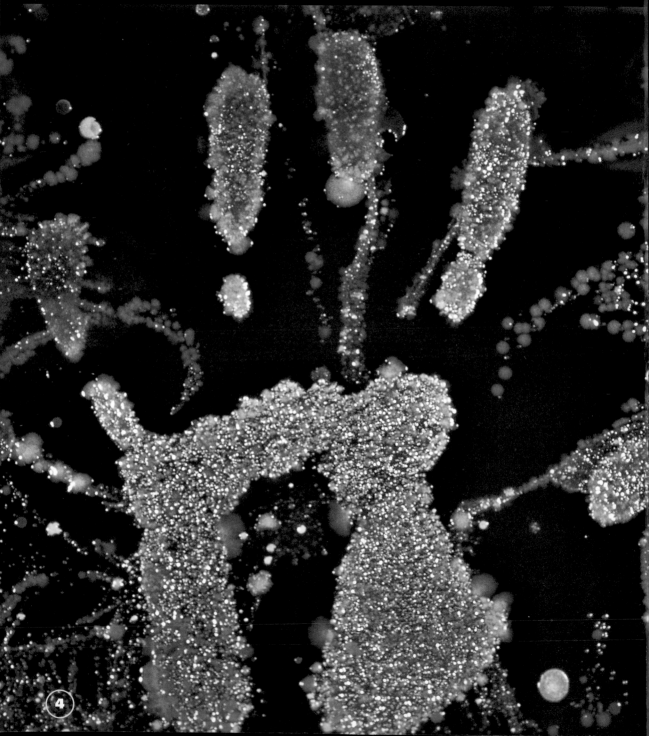

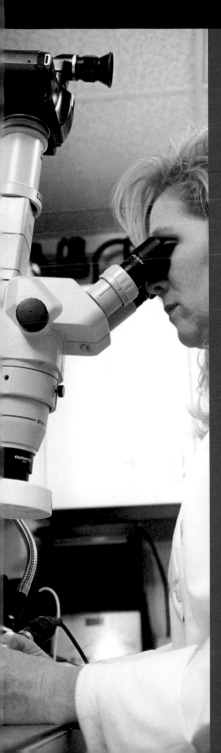

The handprint in the picture is made of germs commonly found on human skin. These germs are so tiny you can't even see them. You can bet that they're there, though ... and this handprint proves it.

How was it made? A person's hand was pressed down onto a plate containing nutrients that germs feed on. After the hand was removed, germs too small to see were left behind. The germs were allowed to multiply and grow. Soon the telltale shape of a human hand came into view.

We are exposed to billions of germs every day. They live all around us. Some even live on us and in us. Yet most of us are healthy human beings. Why aren't we sick all the time?

The simple answer is that our bodies have their own systems of protection. Fortunately, medical research is helping us out. But fighting disease is a constant battle. Today, we are in a much better position to win than ever before.

Chapter 1

Your Body's Lines of Defense

The year was 1906. Several members of a New York family mysteriously fell ill. A new cook had just been hired. People began to wonder. Was the new cook poisoning the family's food?

As it turned out, Mary Mallon, the cook, was guilty—but not in the way you might think! The family had a disease called typhoid fever. This disease travels from person to person through water or food. Although Mary did not appear to be sick, she was a carrier of the typhoid germ, shown below. Without knowing it, Mary was spreading the disease to other people when she prepared their food.

So how can we protect ourselves from things we can't even see? Luckily, our bodies have natural lines of defense. We also have medicines that help our body's defense systems work even better. Today **vaccines** protect us from typhoid and many other diseases.

It's important to understand what causes disease and how our bodies fight disease. There are many things we can do to protect ourselves and stay healthy.

What do eating well, sneezing, and washing your hands have in common?

The germ that causes typhoid fever (greatly enlarged)

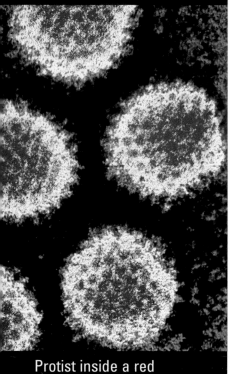

Adenovirus, a type of virus that causes the common cold

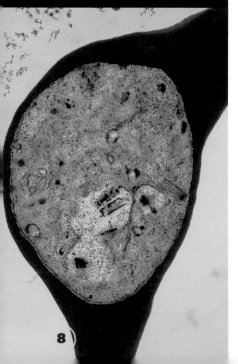

Protist inside a red blood cell infected with malaria

Some Diseases Can Spread

Have you ever noticed how colds seem to spread quickly from just one person? One day your friend is sneezing. A few days later you start to sniffle. Then a younger brother or sister gets a runny nose. Soon it seems that everyone in your home is reaching for a tissue. Why does this happen?

It happens because a cold is a **communicable disease**. It is an illness that can spread from person to person. Communicable diseases are caused by **pathogens**—what most people think of as germs. Pathogens include viruses, some bacteria, protists, fungi, and even some parasites. Most of these pathogens are too small to be seen with the human eye. We can see many of them only by looking at them under a microscope.

Viruses

The pathogens that cause diseases such as influenza (the flu) and the common cold are **viruses**. Viruses are extremely small and are not even considered living organisms. Viruses cannot reproduce on their own. They have to invade a living cell and take it over to make more viruses.

Bacteria

They live all around us in the air, water, and soil. Some bacteria are actually helpful to humans. Other kinds of bacteria are harmful. Harmful bacteria act as pathogens in the human body and can make us sick. **Bacteria** are very small and can reproduce quickly. The streptococci bacteria, at right, have been magnified more than 6,500 times so that they can be seen clearly.

Protists

Many **protists** do not harm humans, but some are pathogens that can make you ill. In the image on the bottom of page 8, the green area pictures a protist invading a red blood cell (dark red area). This protist causes the disease malaria. Mosquitoes can carry these pathogens. When an infected female mosquito bites a person, the protists can move from the mosquito into its victim's bloodstream. Most cases of malaria occur in tropical countries.

Fungi

Most **fungi** are either helpful or harmless to humans. However, a few act as pathogens. Some of those cause skin infections. If you have ever felt the itch of athlete's foot, you know what a fungus can do.

Parasites

Some organisms, called **parasites**, get their energy by feeding on other living things. The tapeworm in the picture to the right is a parasite. It lives inside a person's intestines where it takes nutrients directly from food the person ate. This parasite is one pathogen that can grow very long. Some tapeworms can measure up to 9 meters (30 feet) long.

Bacteria that cause strep throat

Fungi (orange) that cause skin infections, such as athlete's foot

Tapeworm, a parasite that can cause intestinal and other problems

What if...?

Researchers are working on a "smart bandage." This bandage will contain a tiny sensor able to identify germs in a wound. What if you cut yourself? How do you think this bandage would help you avoid an infection?

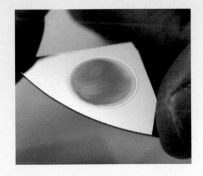

Natural Defenses

What can you do to protect yourself from these pathogens? Lucky for you, your body has several lines of defense to help you avoid disease. Your body's system of fighting disease is called the **immune system**. It is hard at work 24 hours a day. You don't even have to think about it to make it work. The immune system's main job is to protect you from communicable diseases. How does your body protect you?

One of your body's best ways of fighting disease is to keep pathogens from ever getting inside your body. The largest organ of your body is part of this first line of defense. What is this organ? It's your skin. Most pathogens can't get through skin unless the skin is broken. Can you guess why it's important to keep a cut or scrape clean?

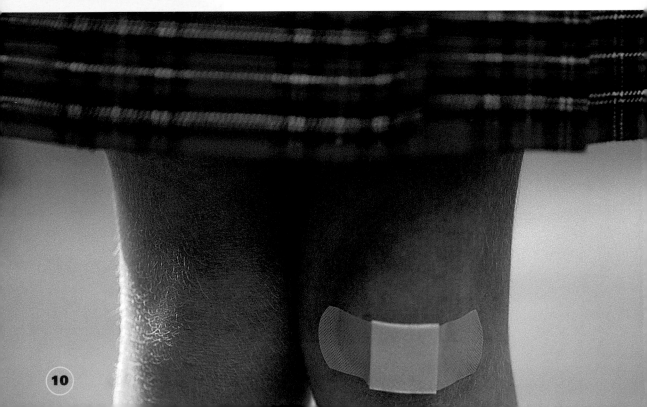

Pathogens also invade your body through other openings, such as your nose and mouth. What does your body do when this happens? Here's a hint: "Achoo!" That's right, when you sneeze, your body is helping to protect you.

Just think about a sneeze. You sniff and a chain reaction begins. Something irritates the hairs in your nose. The hairs activate nerve cells. The cells send a message to your brain. In a split second, your brain sends an order to your chest muscles to sneeze. As you "achoo," air speeds out of your body at up to 160 kilometers (100 miles) an hour. **Mucus** and germs also fire out of your body as you sneeze.

You barely have time to think about a sneeze. It is your body's immediate response to protect you. The sticky mucus lining in your nose and throat helps trap pathogens. Then your body gets rid of them when you cough or sneeze.

Tears and saliva are part of your immune system. If dust carries pathogens into your eyes, tears often wash them away. If you eat something with pathogens in it, your saliva can protect you. Saliva, along with the digestive juices in the stomach, can kill pathogens.

Your body has many ways to keep pathogens out. Sometimes, however, they manage to get through the first lines of defense. When this happens, pathogens take up residence in your body and make you sick.

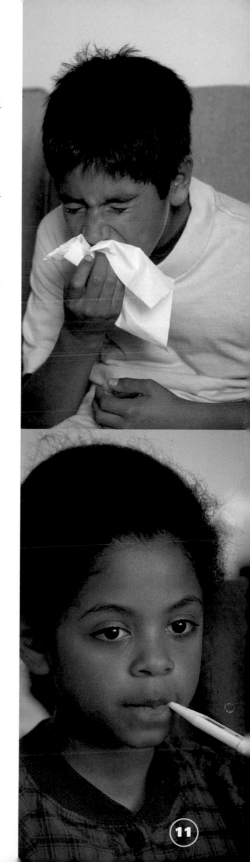

Stay Tuned!

Does chicken soup cure a cold? Medical research says probably not. However, eating chicken soup seems to make people feel better. So maybe it's worth a bowl or two. Researchers are still working on a cure for the common cold. Stay tuned to see what happens!

Attacking the Pathogens

Don't think the fight is over when you get sick. In fact, the battle in your body is probably just beginning. When pathogens find their way into your body, white blood cells come to the rescue. The **lymphatic system** helps produce and move these cells throughout your body. The vessels that make up the lymphatic system carry a clear fluid called **lymph**. This fluid has seeped out of blood vessels and contains many white blood cells.

To see how white blood cells defend the body, let's look at what happens when you catch a cold. When a cold virus successfully invades your nose, chemicals are released to tell your body something is wrong. This starts a chain of events that brings many white blood cells to the scene to destroy the viruses.

As white blood cells move from the lymph system to the area where the virus was found, the lining of your nose often swells. More mucus is produced. This makes it harder for you to breathe. You get a stuffed-up feeling. The good news about all that discomfort is that it means your immune system is hard at work.

What are some other signs that show your body is fighting the cold virus?

The lymphatic system is a body system that helps us fight disease. This network is made up of nodes, small vessels, and organs, such as the spleen and tonsils (not shown).

Lymphatic System

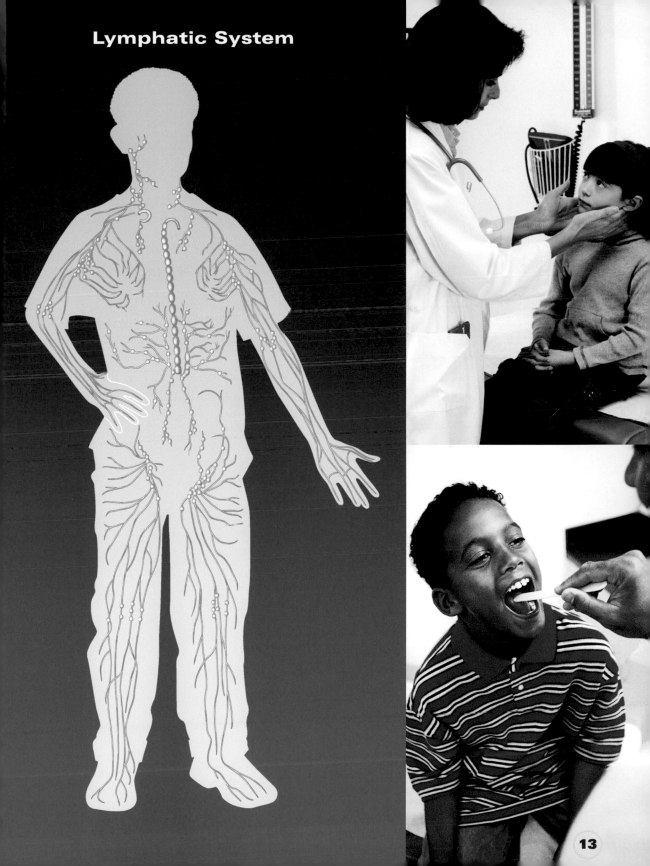

The young woman in the pink T-shirt carried a measles virus to her college campus. All of the college students in the picture got sick from it. The good news is that now they probably all have immunity against the measles virus.

Antibodies and Immunity

Your body reacts to pathogens in many different ways. Specialized white blood cells are able to recognize different types of pathogens. They produce chemicals that fight them. Sometimes certain white blood cells produce **antibodies**. The antibodies attach themselves to specific pathogens and weaken them. As the number of antibodies increases, the pathogens become targets for white blood cells to destroy.

Have you ever had chicken pox? If so, you've probably gotten it only once. Why? It's because your immune system has memory cells. If you are infected with the chicken pox virus again, your immune system recognizes the pathogen. Then your immune system can quickly make antibodies to protect you. These antibodies give you **immunity**, or resistance, to protect you from getting sick again.

So if antibodies protect you, why do you keep getting sick with colds year after year? Your body may have produced antibodies against *particular* cold viruses. But there are hundreds of different types of viruses that cause the common cold. You don't have antibodies against them all. So every time a new type infects your body, you get sick and you produce new antibodies against that particular type of virus. Another problem is that a cold virus can change to form new kinds of viruses. So the immune system has to keep working to produce new kinds of antibodies against whatever pathogens show up.

Some Diseases Do Not Spread

Diseases that are not typically spread from person to person are called **noncommunicable diseases**. They have a variety of causes. Some are caused by a malfunction in the body. Some are caused by environmental conditions or poor health habits. Some noncommunicable diseases are inherited, or passed down from one generation to the next.

Sometimes the immune system is the cause of the disease. Juvenile diabetes is one example of a noncommunicable disease caused by a mistake in the immune system. In this kind of diabetes a person's immune system destroys certain cells that produce insulin. Insulin is a chemical that helps the body control the sugar level in the blood.

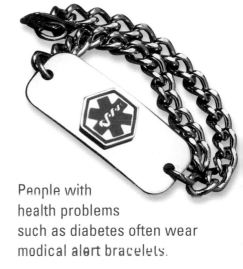

People with health problems such as diabetes often wear medical alert bracelets.

Using water from polluted rivers, such as this one in Nepal, can increase a person's risk of getting cancer and other noncommunicable diseases.

Chapter 2

Medical Breakthroughs

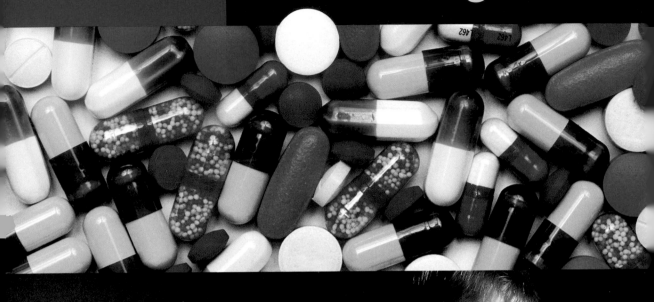

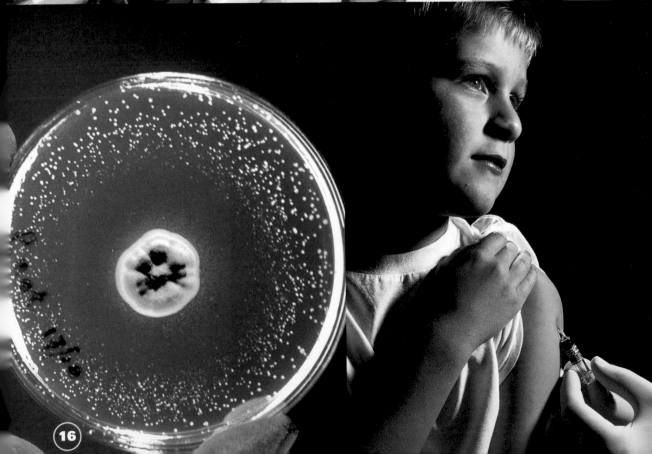

It was 1796. An English doctor was about to perform a daring experiment. He was going to expose a healthy eight-year-old boy named James Phipps to the deadly smallpox virus. Why would a doctor do such a thing?

Edward Jenner was about to prove that vaccines could protect humans against certain diseases. Dr. Jenner had noticed that milkmaids did not often get smallpox. They did, however, catch cowpox from the cows they milked. Cowpox is a mild disease that causes sores on the hands. The milkmaids usually recovered completely. Jenner had scratched some cowpox matter from a milkmaid's infected hand into James Phipps's arm two months earlier. The boy came down with cowpox, but he recovered. Now Dr. Jenner scratched smallpox matter into the boy's arm. Amazingly, James stayed healthy.

No one, including Jenner, understood exactly why his experiment worked. At that time people did not know much about pathogens and antibodies. But cowpox and smallpox are similar diseases. So the antibodies developed against cowpox actually worked to protect people against smallpox, a more serious and often deadly disease.

Today we know that medicines can sometimes help our immune system keep us healthy. Read on to find out how a shot in the arm can give you a leg up on disease!

Louis Pasteur developed a vaccine for rabies.

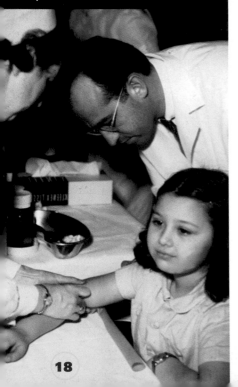

Jonas Salk watches as a girl receives the polio vaccine.

Vaccines

Almost one hundred years after Jenner's experiment, another scientist was working with a different kind of vaccine. His name was Louis Pasteur, and he was a famous French chemist. In 1885 Pasteur isolated a weak form of a rabies virus in rabbits. Rabies is a fatal disease that spreads to people through the bite of an infected animal. When an animal with rabies bit nine-year-old Joseph Meister, most people thought the young boy would die. Louis Pasteur tried to save him. He gave the boy a series of shots using bits of tissue from a rabbit that had died from rabies. Joseph Meister did not get sick. The vaccine saved him. It had transferred antibodies from the rabbit to his own immune system.

Vaccines don't make us sick. Vaccines give our immune system the information it needs to make antibodies and memory cells. This way the body is prepared to fight off certain pathogens before we ever have to get sick from them.

Most Americans get vaccines, especially children. In fact, you can't even start school in the United States without having certain vaccinations. Why? Because vaccinations help our immune systems prevent disease. For example, polio is a disease that can paralyze limbs and, in severe cases, cause death. In the early 1950s more than 20,000 cases of polio occurred in the United States each year. In 1955 a polio vaccine developed by Jonas Salk became available. Since then, millions of children have been vaccinated. Today the United States and many other countries worldwide are polio-free.

Magic Bullets

In the early 20th century researchers discovered **antibiotics**. Antibiotics are substances that kill or stop the growth of harmful bacteria and other organisms. Scientists had known that there were many substances that could kill dangerous bacteria in our bodies. The problem was that those substances also damaged healthy cells along with the pathogen. Could scientists find "magic bullets" that would destroy only the bacteria and leave the rest of the body cells alone?

In the 1920s a Scottish scientist named Alexander Fleming discovered one of these "magic bullets." He was growing bacteria in his research lab. He observed that bacteria in one of the petri dishes (see the dish on page 16) did not grow around a certain mold. The mold turned out to be a powerful bacteria killer. From this mold, the first antibiotic—called penicillin—was developed. It changed medical science forever.

Alexander Fleming, a bacteriologist, works in his lab.

Thinking Like a Scientist:

Hypothesizing

When scientists ask a question and make a good guess at what the answer might be, they are **hypothesizing**. For example, early researchers hypothesized that there was a substance that could kill bacteria while leaving healthy cells alone. They then tested the hypothesis. They performed many experiments before finding a substance that killed bacteria and proved the hypothesis true.

Scientists may also find that a hypothesis is not true. Sometimes they learn just as much from an experiment that shows a hypothesis is *not* true as from an experiment that shows a hypothesis is true. What do you think a scientist can learn from a hypothesis that has been proven wrong?

Attacking Invaders

Your skin, tears, sweat, and the mucus lining in your nose and throat are the body's first lines of defense against disease. Their job is to keep pathogens from entering your body. However, pathogens sometimes get past the first lines of defense and invade body tissue. When that happens, the second line of defense—**the inflammatory response**—begins. Here's how it works.

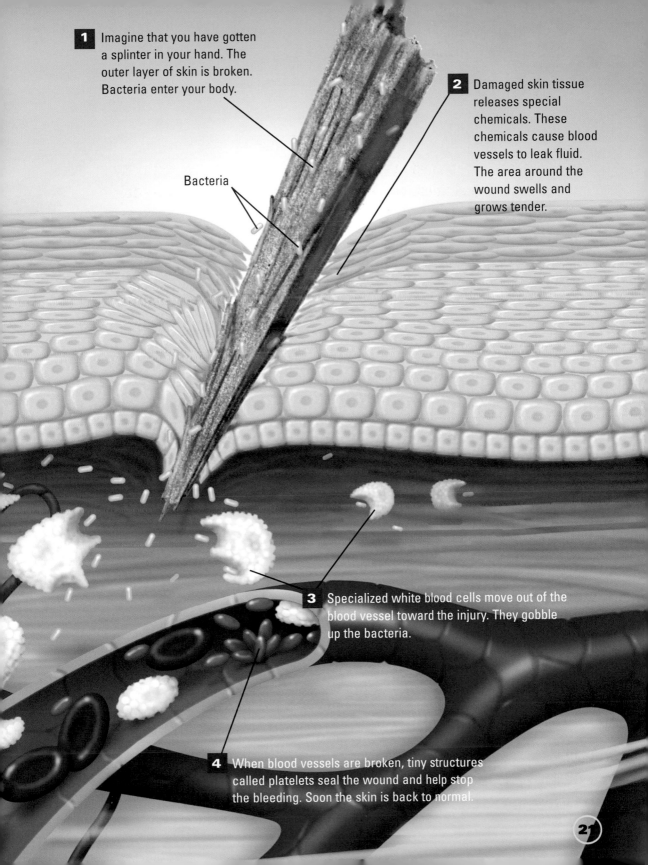

1 Imagine that you have gotten a splinter in your hand. The outer layer of skin is broken. Bacteria enter your body.

Bacteria

2 Damaged skin tissue releases special chemicals. These chemicals cause blood vessels to leak fluid. The area around the wound swells and grows tender.

3 Specialized white blood cells move out of the blood vessel toward the injury. They gobble up the bacteria.

4 When blood vessels are broken, tiny structures called platelets seal the wound and help stop the bleeding. Soon the skin is back to normal.

Chapter 3

New Discoveries, Longer Lives

It was April 12, 1999. Matthew Scott and his son were celebrating. Mr. Scott had just thrown the honorary first pitch at the Philadelphia Phillies opening baseball game. What was so special about this event? Mr. Scott threw the ball with a hand that was not his own.

Matthew Scott was the first person in the United States to receive a successful hand **transplant**. He had lost his own hand in an accident, but doctors were able to attach a new hand from a donor. The operation took more than 14 hours. Doctors were able to attach all the muscles, blood vessels, and skin from the donor's hand. Although the surgery went well, one big problem remained.

The donor hand was not made of Scott's own body cells. The immune system attacks any foreign, or unfamiliar, object in the body. Doctors knew that Scott's immune system would try to destroy the new organ. How could they prevent that from happening?

Matthew Scott was given anti-rejection medication. In the last 20 years researchers have developed powerful new drugs that can turn a person's immune system off. Some of these drugs can help people recover when an organ is transplanted from one person to another. The drugs also help the body to accept the new organ.

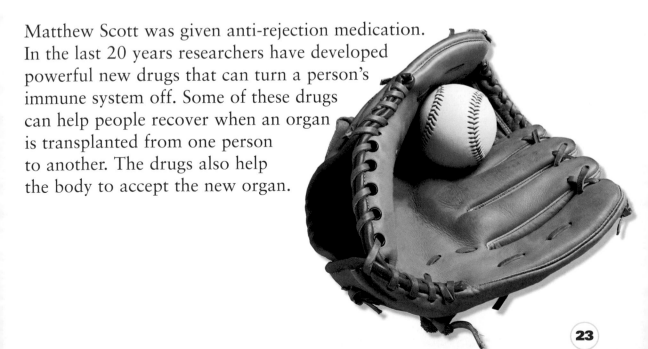

Controlling the Immune System

Lifesaving transplant operations have successfully delivered hearts, lungs, and other body parts to thousands of people who needed them. However, many transplant patients need to stay on medication that controls their immune system for the rest of their lives. This medication can have serious side effects that make people sick. In addition to keeping the immune system from attacking the transplanted body part, the drugs keep the immune system from attacking pathogens that invade the body. As a result, people who get transplants often suffer from other, sometimes deadly, infections.

Changing the Instructions

Researchers today are looking for new ways to control the immune response. In transplant cases, scientists want to turn off only the part of the immune system that is trying to reject the new organ. This would leave the rest of the immune system working to protect the patient.

In other cases, scientists are trying to boost immune response. **Acquired immune deficiency syndrome (AIDS)** is a condition in which the body's immune system is weakened. This means a person has little protection against infections. Scientists are working on a variety of ways that might help restore these weakened immune systems.

Each panel of the AIDS quilt was handstitched in memory of someone who died of AIDS.

Looking Ahead

Immune system research is at a very exciting stage. There have been many breakthroughs, but much remains to be done. Just think of all the possibilities. As we learn more about the human body and disease, we will be able to prevent more illness. Someday we may even be able to cure diseases such as AIDS and cancer. Some cancer researchers think the body may fight cancer in much the same way it fights disease-causing viruses. Researchers continue to study the immune system to find more ways to help the body fight cancer and other diseases.

Advances in medicine are making it possible for babies born today to have a brighter future. Who knows how much longer and healthier their lives will be due to new discoveries on the horizon!

Word Power

The word *antibiotic* comes from the Greek words *anti,* meaning "against," and *bios,* meaning "life."

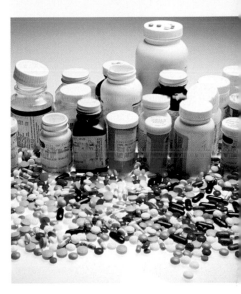

Hypothesizing

Think of all the questions you ask every day. Curiosity about the things around you helps you learn and understand. When scientists have a problem they often ask questions. Then they form a hypothesis as an answer. A hypothesis is an educated guess about an outcome. A good hypothesis can be tested. The test will show whether the hypothesis is true or not.

Sometimes people get allergies. This means their immune system overreacts to harmless substances. Anita went to the doctor with itchy eyes, a runny nose, sneezing, and coughing. Her symptoms had gone on for many weeks starting in late summer. Her doctor suspected she had an allergy. He hypothesized that Anita might be allergic to ragweed. Ragweed pollen, dustlike grains released by the plant, appear in the air mainly in late summer and fall.

To test his hypothesis, the doctor made tiny scratches on Anita's arm. He then applied to each scratch a small amount of a substance that might be causing Anita's allergy attack. If a small swelling appeared at the scratch, that would mean that Anita was probably allergic to that substance. The results of Anita's tests are shown in the chart at left.

Substance	Result
Mold	none
Ragweed pollen	none
Pet dander (flakes from dog or cat skin)	swelling
House dust	none

Practice the Skill

1. Was the doctor's hypothesis correct?

2. What might be causing Anita's allergy symptoms?

Check It Out

What questions would you ask next if you were Anita's doctor?

Gertrude Belle Elion: Drug Discoverer

Gertrude Belle Elion was a chemist who helped create important drugs to treat many serious diseases. She hypothesized that growth and reproduction in diseased cells would be different from growth and reproduction in normal cells. Her research helped her to develop some new approaches to drug design. In 1988 Elion and two other researchers were awarded the Nobel Prize in Medicine for their discoveries of important principles in drug treatment.

Hands-on Science

Modeling How Disease Spreads

Pathogens get passed around. Just the simple act of shaking hands can spread pathogens to many people. Try this activity to see how germs get around.

Materials

✔ Glitter
✔ 1 sheet of dark construction paper
✔ Hand lens (optional)

Explore

1 Work in groups of six.

2 Sprinkle some glitter on a sheet of dark construction paper.

3 Have one student lightly place his or her right hand on the glitter.

4 The student with the glitter should shake hands with student 2.

5 Student 2 should then shake hands with student 3.

6 Student 3 should shake hands with student 4.

7 Student 4 should shake hands with student 5.

8 Student 5 should shake hands with student 6.

9 Now study everybody's right hand. You may need a hand lens. What do you see?

Think

The glitter represents germs. Describe how germs spread from one person to another.

How do you think washing your hands helps stop the spread of germs?

Can you think of other ways that germs can get on hands?

Science Notebook

The best line of defense is prevention. So, here are some ways you can keep healthy.

- Eat healthy foods.
- Get enough sleep.
- Exercise.
- Avoid tobacco, alcohol, and drugs.
- Keep a positive attitude.
- Enjoy some relaxing music. Believe it or not, one experiment showed that "easy listening" music raised the levels of antibodies in some people.
- Laugh! Another study showed that college students who listened to humorous tapes had higher antibody levels than those who listened to a lecture.

Websites to Visit

http://www.brainpop.com
Visit this site to find animated movies on a variety of health and science topics, including the immune system.

http://newscenter.cancer.gov
The National Cancer Institute gives background information on a wide range of science issues covered in the news.

Books to Read

Anderson, Laurie Halse. *Fever 1793*. Simon & Schuster, 2000. This historical fiction tells the story of how one family coped with an epidemic of yellow fever that struck Philadelphia in 1793.

Balkwill, Frances. *Cell Wars (Cells and Things)*. Carolrhoda Books, 1993. Easy-to-read text and colorful illustrations show how the human body fights off pathogens.

Giblin, James Cross, and David Frampton. *When Plague Strikes: The Black Death, Smallpox, AIDS*. HarperTrophy, 1997. This book presents the origins, causes, symptoms, and effects of each disease.

Glossary

acquired immune deficiency syndrome (AIDS) – disease of the immune system caused by the human immunodeficiency virus (HIV)

antibiotic *(an-ti-bye-AHT-ik)* – a drug that can kill or stop the growth of harmful bacteria and other microorganisms

antibody – a substance produced by the body that attaches to a pathogen and aids in its destruction

bacterium *(bak-TIR-ee-um)* – the smallest and simplest of all one-celled microorganisms. Some **bacteria** (plural) cause disease.

communicable disease – disease caused by a pathogen that can spread easily from person to person

fungus *(FUHNG-guhs)* – an organism such as a mold that lives by absorbing nutrients from its surroundings. Some **fungi** (plural) cause disease.

hypothesize *(hye-PAHTH-uh-size)* – to give a possible explanation for an event or something observed

immune system *(i-MYOON sis-tuhm)* all the cells, tissues, and organs that work to protect the body from disease

immunity – ability of the body to defend itself against disease

inflammatory response – the body's second line of defense against pathogens invading through tissue damaged by injury or infection

lymph *(limf)* – clear fluid carried by vessels that make up the lymphatic system. Lymph contains many white blood cells that help fight disease.

lymphatic system *(lim-FAT-ik sis-tuhm)* – a network of vessels that carries lymph and produces and transports white blood cells throughout the body

mucus *(MYOO-kuhs)* – thick, slimy fluid that coats the lining of the nose, mouth, throat, and digestive tract

noncommunicable disease – disease that does not typically spread from person to person

parasite *(PAR-uh-site)* – organism that lives and feeds off another organism

pathogen *(PATH-uh-juhn)* – a substance or living thing that causes disease

protist *(PROH-tist)* – a one-celled or multicelled organism that has animal-like, plant-like, or fungus-like characteristics. Some protists cause disease.

transplant – transfer of a body part from one site in the body to another, or from one organism to another

vaccine *(vak-SEEN)* – dead or weakened germs that stimulate antibody production to provide immunity against a certain disease

virus *(VYE-ruhs)* – tiny disease-causing structure that can only reproduce inside a living cell

Index